MW01016703

The Ultimate Crash Course Guide to Mastering Golf for Beginners in 30 Minutes or Less!

Disclaimer

No part of this publication may be reproduced or transmitted in any form or by any means, mechanical or electronic, including photocopying or recording, or by any information storage and retrieval system, or transmitted by email without permission in writing from the publisher.

While all attempts and efforts have been made to verify the information held within this publication, neither the author nor the publisher assumes any responsibility for errors, omissions, or opposing interpretations of the content herein.

This book is for entertainment purposes only. The views expressed are those of the author alone, and should not be taken as expert instruction or commands. The reader of this book is responsible for his or her own actions when it comes to reading the book.

Adherence to all applicable laws and regulations, including international, federal, state, and local governing professional licensing, business practices, advertising, and all other aspects of doing business in the US, Canada, or any other jurisdiction is the sole responsibility of the purchaser or reader.

Neither the author nor the publisher assumes any responsibility or liability whatsoever on the behalf of the purchaser or reader of these materials.

Any received slight of any individual or organization is purely unintentional.

Table of Contents

Introduction

First and foremost I want to thank you for downloading the book, "The Ultimate Crash Course Guide to Mastering Golf for Beginners in 30 Minutes or Less."

In this book you will learn how to play golf from the very basics to the more complicated rules. We understand that many sports can be off-putting—when surrounded by professionals, it seems hard to really break into it. Not to worry! We'll run you through getting started on mastering golf.

We'll teach you what to look for when buying clubs, and which clubs you'll need most to get started. We'll also teach you how to properly fill out a score card and set up a shot. Worried about what equipment to buy? We've got you covered here, too—we'll tell you what you need to get started, and what kind of equipment is the best for beginners.

Lastly, we'll cover the common mistakes in golf. We've taken time to write out all of the most annoying mistakes beginners make to help you make a good impression on your first outing in golf—if you happen to have a golf game with a boss or superior, you'll benefit from this knowledge even if you play a terrible game!

So don't worry. Whether you're stressing over what to buy or how to play, or even understanding the golf lingo, this eBook will help you become a master of golf. We've also included a glossary of terms at the back of this book to help you understand anything you might read in this eBook, or hear out on the course!

Thanks again for downloading this book, I hope you enjoy it!

Chapter 1: The Basics of Golf

Golf is an ancient sport steeped in tradition. Often thought of as the sport for the cultured, it's often framed in movies as the sport for the rich and famous—whether it's a main character trying to impress their boss at a game of golf, or just a few guys having a good time on the course, golf has been the sport of choice for thousands of people across decades.

Today, nearly every city in the United States has a golf course. It's an extremely popular and prevalent sport worldwide, played by men (and women) of all ages and skill levels. The very rules of golf are designed to level the playing field even when opponents are extremely mismatched in skill. The idea that golf is a sport for only men is a complete fallacy—women have played golf since its very first inception and proven extremely competent in the sport. Golf as a sport for the elderly is also a misconception; the average age of a professional golfer is only around 32! The only reason this age is so much higher than other sports is golf's reliance on *skill* over *endurance*.

Golf is a sport labeled *"Easy to learn, difficult to master."* Becoming competent at golf can be quite simple, with rapid improvement over only a very short time. Yet golfing at a professional level requires years of hard work. This book is your first step on the road to mastery.

Understanding golf is more than just knowing the rules. To gain a true insight of the sport, we must understand its origins. We'll begin this chapter with a brief history of the sport—where it developed, why it became popular, and where golf stands today. The next chapter will be devoted to the *rules* of golf. For those simply wanting to know how the game is played, skip ahead to the next chapter. However, the murky origins of the sport is a very interesting story that's well worth the read.

The History of Golf

Ball-and-club games have been played by nearly every culture around the world at every point in history. This makes the true origins of golf very difficult to decipher, with different games being introduced, mixed, and reworked over time. The Ancient Romans played a game similar to golf more than two thousand years ago. Called *paganica*, the game was played with bent wooden sticks and a small leather ball. However, in the game, two opposing teams fought to hit a specific target. In truth, the game resembles hockey more closely than golf, but some experts believe paganica was simply the precursor to golf—after its introduction to Northern Europe, the game evolved over time.

The English played an early game called *cambuca* in which the equipment was very much the same as paganica. However, actively opposing teams were more or less replaced by alternating players who tried to get their ball to a certain marker before the other.

What historians do agree on is that the defining characteristic of golf—the hole—was first developed by the Scottish in the 1400s. The popularity of their version of the game in which opponents competed to get their ball inside a hole in minimal strokes would wax and wane over time.

> **Watch Out!** Some people think golf was invented by 'barbarous' Scots who would strike the decapitated heads of their enemies into baskets. Though an interesting tale, it's not likely true—not only because recorded history says otherwise, but due to the improbability of trying to hit a 10 pound human head with the aerodynamics of a porcupine into a basket more than a few feet away.

Originally, the popularity of golf was thought of as a danger to the military discipline of the Scottish army. Outlawed by two kings (James II and James IV), it was eventually accepted in Scotland around 1500.

The game gained popularity with the aristocracy in the beginning, thanks largely to the vast amount of wealth and free time they had at their disposal. The connection between golf and the higher class never truly went away—hence the idea we have today of golf being a sport for the cultured and wealthy.

Golf in the 1600s
The first dedicated golf club and golf ball makers were officially sanctioned in the 1600s, around the time golf finally gained traction

in England. The rise of the sport in England is attributable to King James VI, a Scottish noble who took to the throne of England in 1603.

Despite (or because of) the popularity among the upper class, over time golf became popular with the lower classes of Scotland and England, too. However, fields of play were much different between the two. Nobles played on golf courses not very much different from what we have today; not as organized, perhaps, but well maintained and manicured courses were paid for by the elite. The lower classes, in comparison, played on open land amidst trees, shrubs, and even livestock. It could be said that these obstacles helped bring about the common golf course obstacles we see today.

Golf as a Modern Game

After nearly two hundred years of play, golf finally began to take a more recognizable form. The general feeling of exclusivity of the sport remained, however. Around 1800, clubs for golfers were founded with strict limits on members. These golf clubs accepted mostly upper class gentlemen and would, over time, create rules almost identical to what we see in the modern game today.

The oldest club in the world, the *Honourable Company of Edinburgh Golfers*, was founded in 1744 and helped set the standards for modern golf.

The 1800s was the true period of birth for the game of golf. Huge advances in equipment was made during this time, and the popularity of golf finally spread outside of the English Isles and into mainland Europe. Formerly made of leather and feathers, golf balls began to utilize the rubbery sap of the tropical *gutta* tree—they became cheaper and easier to make, which helped popularize the sport with lower classes.

> **Did You Know?** Golf balls are dimpled thanks to observations made after the introduction of the rubber-like *gutta* balls. Golf players noticed that over time, balls that were reused would fly farther than new balls. While the new balls were smooth in nature, older, used balls were covered in dents and divots caused by repeated strikes. Eventually, these divots were worked into manufacturer molds—as it turned out, they reduced drag on the ball by disrupting the airflow. In flight, the air would strike the ball's divots and become chaotic. These

chaotic layers of air around the surface of the ball actually acted as a buffer between the ball's surface and the faster flowing air around it, leading to faster ball speeds and farther strikes!

While wooden clubs had been the major tool of use in golf before the 1800s, the stiffer *gutta* balls required tougher golf clubs, too. Soft wood clubs disappeared entirely, replaced by hardwood clubs protected by leather as well as iron clubs.

The *Open Championship* or *British Open* was created in 1860 which helped to separate amateurs from the professionals. As participation rose, prize money was eventually awarded and 'professional golfing' was born.

Golf in America would take longer still to gain enough popularity for its own governing body and championship to form. It wasn't until about 1900 that America's first tournament, the *U.S. Open* was held. However, once the sport had gained a foothold, it quickly became a favorite pastime for American's nationwide.

Chapter 2: Rules of the Game

Playing golf isn't nearly as difficult as you may think. The rules are simple to follow, and will help save you from embarrassment when playing with friends. Understanding the rules is also important to keep games consistent and fair.

Etiquette and General Rules of Golf

Like every sport, golf requires a certain amount of etiquette between players. Sore losers, cheaters, and poor sports can be found in every sport—you may even play against some yourself. But having the right attitude is important. Proper etiquette can make up for lack of skill, and may just see you invited back another time simply for your polite play.

When it comes to **attitude**, be courteous to all players whether they're on your team or not. Remember *people play at different speeds*. If you're playing too slowly, offer a faster group to play ahead. They won't have to wait for you to play, and you'll get a chance to play at your own speed.

Respect the green; if you damage the grass, take care to repair what you've done. Everyone has to use the same golf course, and no one enjoys playing on a damaged field (or repairing someone else's damage!)

Before playing, **read the course rules**. Often, courses have specific rules and regulations that differ from one another, especially in terms of etiquette. **Keep balls marked** so you can find yours easily (if you're unsure which ball is yours after being hit, it's officially lost). And of course, you can only bring fourteen clubs to play.

During your round, **do not ask advice from your opponent**. Doing so results in penalization. Only your teammates and caddie can give advice. However, simple information is fine (rule clarification, location of hazards, distances on the course, etc.).

Use only regulated equipment. No one wants to see a beginner come to the course with the latest and greatest technology in cheating.

When finished, make sure your scorecard is filled out (in stroke play) or the score gets posted (in match play).

Match Play and Stroke Play

During **match play**, each hole played is a *win* or *lose*. When you have one win more than your opponent, you're considered "one up." Two wins would make you "two up", and so on.

If you have won the majority of holes (two of three holes, three of five holes, etc.), then you needn't play the rest of the course, as you are the winner!

During **stroke play**, the player with the lowest score is the winner. Balls must be hit into the hole before moving onto the next.

The Score Card

On a score card, hole numbers are listed horizontally as the column headers. Scorecards also typically list the *par* (average strokes to get your ball into the hole), as well as common handicaps for the hole. Scores are recorded below this. The larger numbers you see on the scorecard are the distances to the hole.

Below each hole number, you write the number of strokes you took to complete the hole. If under par, circle your score. If over par, draw a square around it.

Golf courses are eighteen holes. Typically, scores are recorded for the first nine holes (the back nine) and then separately for the last nine (front nine). Add the scores to get your final score.

Order of Play

When playing golf, you must decide who is to play first. **During match play, the first player is decided by chance** (tossing a coin, for example). Some players allow the one with the lowest handicap to play first, but the official rules of golf make no mention of this. Generally, after the first hole, **the player with the lowest total score goes first** (the player that is in the lead) at the next hole. **In stroke player, order doesn't matter.**

Although not commonly known, it's worth noting that despite many players not enforcing play order in match play, there do exist penalties. In match play and *only* in match play, an opponent may order a player who has played out of turn to immediately cancel their out-of-turn stroke and play in the correct order, with the ball placed as nearly as possible to the original location.

Did You Know? In the 2000 Solheim Cup, pro golfer Annika Sorenstam was brought to tears when her opponent enforced the above rule, making Sorenstam replay the shot she had just taken.

After the initial strike of match or stroke play, the ball farthest from the hole is played.

The Tee Shot

Place the tee and ball between the tee-markers and up to two club lengths behind them. This area is referred to as the *teeing ground*, a square that is two club lengths in each direction with its forward edge being defined by the placement of the tee-markers. In match play, a tee-off from outside this area must be replayed immediately if the opponent asks. In stroke play, a two stroke penalty is applied (your score is increased by two strokes) *and* the ball must be replayed from within the teeing off area.

After the First Strike

Identifying your ball is important. If you're unsure whether the ball is yours, tell your opponent before marking its position and then physically checking the ball. Balls must be played as they lie. Don't improve your location by flattening, breaking, or moving aside any obstacles unless said obstacles are blocking your swing.

Playing a ball that isn't yours will result in losing the match for that hole during match play, or a two stroke penalty in stroke play.

At the Hole

The area around the hole is designated the *putting green*. Like putt-putt, this area is reserved for short strokes with the appropriate club (a putter).

In this area, balls can be cleaned if replaced in the same spot. The flagstick must also be removed during play at the putting green.

Movement of the Ball

Generally, golf balls must be played as they lie. If *you* accidentally touch or move the ball, a penalty stroke must be applied and the ball replaced to its original position.

However, if an outside agent (someone besides the people at play) move the ball, or another ball causes yours to move, it can be put back in its original position without penalty.

Finally, if your ball is moved by a natural occurrence such as wind or the lay of the land, then it needn't be replaced and can be played where it is.

Lifting Your Golf Ball

When checking or cleaning your golf ball, you must follow the rules in marking, picking up, and dropping the ball.

It's good form to always mark the ball's location before interfering with it, regardless of the requirement to do so (certain situations don't require marking the ball location).

After checking or cleaning, stand up and hold the ball out at shoulder height. Then, drop the ball onto its original position. The ball doesn't have to come to rest at the original location, but only be dropped onto it.

Re-dropping must occur in the follow situations after dropping:

- A ball previously in a hazard comes to a stop outside of it
- A ball previously outside a hazard comes to a stop inside of one
- A ball previously outside the putting green comes to a stop inside of it
- A ball previously inbounds rolls out of bounds
- A ball rolls back into a **condition** (some hazard not designated part of the course)
- A ball comes to rest nearer the hole than its original position
- A ball travels more than two club lengths from its marked location

Playing the Ball As It Doesn't Lie

Balls must be played as they lie except in some circumstances.

When **loose impediments** such as leaves and twigs interfere, they can be moved. If you think a ball might interfere or benefit your play or your opponents play, you may ask for that ball to be lifted.

When a **moveable obstruction** interferes, you may move it. If your ball happens to be on (or in) that obstruction, you may lift the ball, move the obstruction, then replace the ball in approximately the same location.

If an **immovable obstruction** interferes with play, you may drop your ball within a single club-length from it. Examples might be damage to the course made by wild animals, a building, or casual water. However, it cannot be dropped closer to the hole than the nearest point of relief (area of locally raised ground).

If your ball falls into a **water hazard,** you may play the ball as it lies (when inside the boundaries of the hazard but not, obviously, when it's under water). You can accept a one-stroke penalty and re-play the ball from its original location. It can also be placed at the border of the hazard along its original trajectory.

Losing Your Ball
Balls are considered lost if they cannot be found *or* if the ball lands out of bounds of the course. If lost, you must re-play the ball from its original location and accept a one-stroke penalty.

Searching for the ball cannot exceed **five minutes**. However, if you believe your ball has been lost after striking it, you may immediately play a **provisional ball** (after declaring it as such) *before searching for your ball.* If you first ball was indeed lost, a penalty of one stroke is applied and play continues with your provisional ball. If you find your lost ball, you may disregard the provisional ball.

Unplayable Balls
By accepting a penalty of one stroke, you can play any ball from its original location at the time of you shot if you believe it landed in an unplayable area, or it can be played within two club lengths of its current location that doesn't place it nearer to the hole. However, this rule doesn't apply to water hazards (see: *Playing the Ball As It Doesn't Lie*).

What is a Handicap?

The handicap system helps to level the playing field across all experience levels. In simple terms, the handicap is the number of strokes subtracted from the player's score. However, the handicap will change with the player's ability. More experience players will receive smaller handicaps. In cases of the best golfers, their handicap is zero.

> **Did You Know?** Sometimes, the handicap is applied to the player and not the course! Extremely talented players get a *positive* handicap applied to the score. During his prime, Tiger Woods had an amazing handicap of *+10!*

In **stroke play**, a handicap is the number of strokes deducted from his score. The *gross score* is the score without the handicap applied, and the *net score* has the handicap applied.

Let's Play!

With these basic rules of golf in mind, you now have the knowledge to at least get started. But before you go to the golf course, you'll need a few things—primarily, the right equipment. In fact, bringing the *wrong* equipment (shoes included) might find you thrown off the golf course altogether!

Chapter 3: Equipment Buying Guide

We'll start this chapter with one simple rule: beginners shouldn't buy a full set of new clubs. New clubs represent a very large investment of money on your part. As a beginner, you may find that golf just isn't for you and suddenly you're several hundred dollars down. Avoid investing in new clubs until you consistently score below 100 on a standard eighteen hole course. Instead, try buying used clubs. You needn't even have to purchase the full set of fourteen clubs. There are, in fact, *minimalist golfers* who try to play with the fewest clubs possible.

Golf Clubs

The Club Types

At first glance, fourteen golf clubs might seem like overkill. However, the fourteen club rule was actually enacted because some players brought upwards of *twenty* clubs to the golf course! Around the 1930s, the governing bodies for gold in the Americas and Europe decided on a fourteen club limit. Each type of club, and their reason for inclusion, has been described below.

Woods

When trying to hit a ball the farthest distances, woods are the solution. Good golfers can hit a ball 200 to 350 yards! They were originally called woods due to the club heads being made of hardwood. Today, they are made of metal. Woods have flat bottoms with increasing loft (the forward tilt of the clubface when lining up a shot) as the wood number increases. They are referred to as *1-wood*, *2-wood*, etc., with the *1-wood* referred to as the **driver** (used to hit the ball the farthest distances).

Irons

Used for medium distances—200 yards from the hole or less—irons are so named because they were traditionally made from iron. Like woods, irons are now usually made from metals like aluminum and titanium. Irons are named from one to nine (*1-iron*, *2-iron*, up to the *9-iron*) and, like the woods, increase in loft as the number increases.

Irons *1* through *3* are **long irons**, sending the ball the farthest of the nine. **Middle irons** consist of irons *4* through *6* and used when 150 to 170 yards from the hole, and **short irons** are the remaining three and used to get height with your ball. Typically, irons *1* through *2* are omitted due to their difficulty in use.

Wedges

When your ball becomes stuck in a hazard, the wedge is used to escape. Wedges are good at providing great height to your strike. A **pitching wedge**, like the pitcher in baseball, is used to send your ball both far and high. A **sand wedge**, in comparison, is used to get your ball out of sand hazards (bunkers). A **lob wedge** is good for getting good height but short distance, and a **gap wedge** is used for distances as long as 100 yards. Usually, only **pitching wedges** are included in starter kits.

Putters

Probably the most used golf club, putters are used on the putting green to knock balls short distances over fairly flat terrain. Putters present a very flat surface with which the ball is struck.

Sizing Your Clubs

Like any sports equipment, golf clubs must be sized correctly to be used to greatest affect. Clubs come in 'standard' sizes which may be good for beginning players. Keep in mind that women's clubs are usually one inch shorter than men's.

Shaft length is important as it allows the greatest swing speed *without* lessening the amount of control you have. If you want to purchase clubs suited to your size, we recommend going to any sports store specializing in golf—any competent salesman will be able to take your measurements and inform you of your deviation from standard.

Shaft and Grip

Generally, stiffer shafts are used for players with faster swing speeds. Iron shafts are considered stiff, whereas graphite shafts are considered flexible.

The average distance of your drive can help determine what kind of flex you want in the shaft of your woods. A regular flex shaft is used for the average drive of 200 to 235 yards. Less, and you may consider senior or ladies flex—if your drives travel farther, a stiffer flex (stiff flex or extra-stiff flex) is better.

Irons have similar levels of flex, though in this case it's determined by which iron you use for shots of 150 yards. A *7-iron* is the typical club used for this length shot. Less than a *7-iron* means you need more flex, and greater than a *7-iron* means you need a stiffer shaft.

When trying golf clubs, keep a golf glove on your hand. Medium or medium-large gloves use a standard grip on clubs. Larger gloves use larger grips.

Final Thoughts

Although everyone seems to have advice when choosing the perfect club, the ultimate decider is you. Use whichever clubs feel most comfortable for you, even if your choice is unorthodox. Golf is about relaxing and enjoying oneself. If a certain set of clubs feels most comfortable, then go for it!

A good initial set up should consist of three hybrid clubs numbered *3* to *5* with composite shafts, with irons from the *6-iron* upward (including a pitching wedge) with a steel shaft. Woods should include a driver, a *3-wood*, and a *5-wood*, each with a composite shaft. When branching out, a sand wedge is a good purchase to round out this list.

Choosing a Golf Glove

The best glove material (and most expensive) is leather. Synthetic gloves can also be useful, however, as they provide better grip in wet weather. Hybrid gloves exist for people who want a leather grip without the cost—these gloves have leather in the palm and a synthetic upper.

Gloves should be tight at the palm with only a little give at the fingertips. Pinch the glove to test the fit; pinching should be impossible in the palm and only *just* possible at the fingertips.

When putting on your glove, insert your four fingers first and pull it on tightly. Only then should you insert your thumb.

Golf Shoes

Golf shoes help you keep traction on the course and provide greater power to your swings. A solid stance will greatly increase your drive length.

Sizing Your Shoes

Although it may seem silly, measure *both* feet individually. Often, people discover one foot is half a size or more larger or smaller. Purchase whichever size is larger, or (if possible) purchase a different sized shoe for each foot. Shoes should bend with your foot, in the same place, and be tighter around the middle of your foot. It's the middle of your foot which provides support during a full swing, and so it needs to be tighter. Finally, keep a small gap at the front of your shoe—about an inch from your largest toe to the inside wall.

Material Matters

Cheap shoes will quickly create problems for you. Ideally, you want a shoe that is both breathable and waterproof. Many synthetics aren't breathable. The best shoes you can buy have leather uppers. However, comfort is of utmost importance. If your budget can't make room for it, then choose the shoes you find most comfortable.

Getting the Right Golf Bag

Golf bags are often underrated with the majority of new players unconcerned with which bag they choose. However, there are a multitude of bags available. When buying, consider how many clubs you have, your usual mode of transport when golfing, or other gear you may carry.

Staff Bags

A staff bag is usually out of the question for beginners. A choice for professional golfers, a staff bag is heavy at around ten pounds and very spacious. It can generally fit a full array of clubs and more. If you usually walk the golf course, you'll probably quickly tire of lugging this type of bag around. However, it *is* a very roomy bag and it's usually made of very high quality materials.

Cart Bags

As the name implies, these bags are designed to be carried in a golf cart instead of over the shoulder. They're lighter and smaller than staff bags, but still roomier than other alternatives. If you plan on using a golf cart to traverse the course, this is a good choice.

Carry Bags

Carry bags are the 'common' golf bag you see. They're designed to be carried using an attached shoulder strap. They're smaller than the previous designs, but also much lighter. The average weight of an unfilled carry bag is an astonishing two pounds! Yet carry bags have the least dividers and pockets, usually only splitting the bag into two for your clubs and a smattering of pockets throughout. A regular carry bag is a good choice for beginner due to its versatility.

There exists another type of carry bag, called the **stand bag**, which is the same as a carry bag but includes collapsible legs. These legs keep your bag upright when on the course. They're heavier, but convenient.

How Much is Too Much?

Whether buying a starting kit or purchasing your equipment piecemeal, it can be expensive. The cheapest kits are around $100, but generally the equipment is almost worthless. Once you go beyond renting equipment, you'll want to invest about $500 to get everything together.

Last Notes

Don't concern yourself with having the best or most high tech equipment. In the end, the most important aspect to your gear is reliability and dependability. Shiny clubs mean nothing if they can't help you hit your ball very far. Likewise, golf clubs that essentially hit the ball for you are just as meaningless. Buy, borrow, or rent a decent and dependable set of clubs and a cheap bag to hold them when you start—all other equipment is more or less optional. Then build up your collection slowly as you game improves, filling in gaps with new clubs or replacing clubs you don't find to your liking.

Chapter 4: The Importance of Proper Form

The secret to a powerful swing is proper form. Without it, you'll find yourself committing an embarrassing number of *mulligans*. Getting the stance right takes time and will usually require help from an experienced golfer to tell you what you're doing wrong—it's hard to watch your stance while swinging, unless you happen to record it with a video camera to review afterward!

Getting the Stance Right

You want to stand with your non-dominant side facing the direction you want the ball to go. Keep your front foot slightly ahead of the ball so that your club rests slightly behind the ball. Keep feet slightly more than shoulder width apart. Left-handers can safely flip all of this advice.

You want to be standing about two feet from the ball and bend slightly *at the waist* to bring your golf club head to the ball. The back and arms should remain comfortably straight.

"Keeping your alignment square" refers to the position of your stance. Shoulders and feet should be in line with the target, respectively.

It's very easy to look rigid. However, when taking your stance, try to stay loose and keep your joints slightly bent for a more relaxed, natural look. Lastly, don't favor one foot over the other—stay balanced!

Gripping Your Club

There are many valid ways to hold a golf club and no rules for which to use. In the beginning, use a common and neutral grip. With fingers outstretched, put the top of the golf club shaft into your fingers. The club should extend only half an inch out of your hand. Without closing your grip, the shaft should run from the middle of your index finger to the very base of your pinky finger. Now, close your hand on the shaft, keeping your thumb pad pressed against it.

If you were to hold the club for a swing and look down, you should see only two knuckles on your left hand (index and middle finger knuckles).

Now, you should place the bottom part of your right thumb overtop your left thumb with the pad pressed against the shaft. Your two thumbs should be in line. The webbing between your right thumb and right index finger should point straight up. Close your fingers around the golf club shaft.

Keep your grip relaxed, and be sure to seek advice from professionals as you improve your golf game. A grip can be the different between a 50 yard drive and a 200 yard drive!

Chapter 5: Common Mistakes in Golf

Golf is a very precise game. Small changes can really affect your gameplay and eventual score. Although it looks easy, even hitting the ball can be a difficult task. Hitting it both far *and* at the target isn't anywhere near as easy as it looks—because to do so involves everything from stance to grip to clubs to *attitude*. We've included some of the most common mistakes in golf for you to remember the next time you go golfing.

- **Forgetting the Rules:** As a beginner, you'll probably forget some of the rules while playing. That's all right. But make an effort to remember them and spend time watching others play (on TV or at events) so you have a better understanding.

- **Shooting for a Hole-in-One:** A hole-in-one might amaze your friends, but even the best golfers rarely manage it. Shooting straight for the flag isn't always the best idea if you can't determine where the ball will land. Instead, aim halfway down the green—there's nothing wrong with an average par.

- **Taking Your Time:** It's important to get your shot lined up, but golf courses are shared between other players too. If you find yourself taking too long between shots, invite other players to go ahead of you.

- **Shouting:** To put it simply, stay quiet. Shout after your own ball all you want, but when your partner or opponent is taking a shot, relax. Jeering (and cheering) isn't as polite as staying quiet.

- **Using the Wrong Clubs:** This applies to club length as well as club type. As a beginner, people will understand if your clubs aren't properly sized or you choose the wrong type—you may even benefit from a stranger's kindness who wants to see his old clubs in safe hands! But once you've moved past the beginner stage, get the right clubs for you.

- **Damaging the Course:** Accidents happen. However, you should never walk away after you've damaged the green. Repair any divots you make.

- **"Fore!":** This isn't a stereotype, it's a necessity. If you're in danger of striking someone with your ball, shout *fore* as a warning.

- **No Goal:** If you're hitting the ball without regard for where it lands, you're playing a bad game. Aim your ball toward *something*, preferably a favorable area.

- **Temper Tantrums:** Golf can be played by children, but you shouldn't act like one. Stay calm even when things aren't going your way.

- **Not Keeping an Eye on the Ball:** Why should you keep an eye on your ball? Because you have to go get it. Even if it's a bad shot, watch where it lands so you can retrieve it.

- **Exaggeration:** Remember the fisherman who caught a fish *this big*? Well, no one likes a golfer who hit a ball *this far* either.

- **Bad Dropping:** Know how to drop the ball correctly. It's a common enough task and doing it wrong can be seen as cheating.

- **Whining:** If you're having a bad game, accept it.

- **Too Much Practicing:** Likewise, practicing too much is more or less cheating, too. Don't ask for too many practice shots.

Common mistakes are just that: common. As a beginner, you'll be forgiven for making them, and you will undoubtedly discover more mistakes than we could possibly cover in this book. The most important thing is to learn from them. Don't be offended if someone calls you out for making a mistake—learn from it. The worst player is one who makes the same mistake every time.

And when you become a master of golf, don't be too harsh on the new players either. You'll want a teacher to help guide you in your golf game, after all—so when you're a master, you should go out of your way to help others learn, too. It's all in the spirit of the game.

Conclusion

Thank you again for downloading this book!

I hope this book was able to help you to learn the basics of golf and get you started in playing the game. Again, we've included a glossary of terms at the back of this book if there is any confusion with golf terms while you read or while you play.

The next step upon successful completion of this book is to practice, practice, *practice*. You should never stop practicing to improve your game. It's easy to worry that you're not skilled enough to go out and play, but you will never improve otherwise.

Golfers, like most sports players, are always eager to teach someone the ropes if you make it clear that you're new to the game and interested in learning. Anyone who doesn't want to help isn't worth your time.

The first step to bringing your golf game out to the real world is practicing your stance and hitting the ball. Before going out for a game of golf, try going to a driving range; practicing hitting balls until your hands get blisters. Practice driving balls until you can do it in your sleep. While there, try to meet people who you can play a casual game with once you understand the mechanics of the golf swing.

To master *anything*, you must at first be very, very bad at it. So don't worry if you can't even hit the ball without tossing a lump of dirt after it (although we recommend not playing on a real golf course until you've moved beyond that stage). You'll become a master golfer in no time following the simple steps in this guide. Just relax and have fun—golf is a game all about the right kind of attitude.

Finally, if you enjoyed this book, please take the time to share your thoughts and post a review on Amazon. It'd be greatly appreciated!

Thank you and good luck!

Glossary of Terms

- **Albatross:** A hole played three strokes less than par

- **Approach Shot:** A shot hit from the fairway onto the green

- **Birdie:** A hole played in one stroke less than par

- **Bogey:** A hole played in one stroke *more* than par

- **Bunker:** Sand traps on a golf course

- **Casual Water:** Water not part of the course (rainwater, puddles, etc.)

- **Club Face:** The part of the club which touches the ball

- **Course Handicap:** The number of allowable handicap strokes given per round

- **Divot:** The result of a golf club striking (and damaging) the grass on the course during a swing

- **Dog Leg:** A hole not in line with the course

- **Double Bogey:** A play played in two strokes *more* than par

- **Drive:** a long tee shot usually hit with a driver

- **Eagle:** A hole played in two strokes less than par

- **Fairway:** Short grass between the tee and the green

- **Fore:** Shouted as warning when the ball may strike other plays or spectators

- **Fringe:** Area of medium length grass surrounding the shortest cut grass of the green

- **Green, The:** Area around the hole designed for putting

- **Handicap:** A number representing the golfer's playing skill. The lower the handicap, the more skilled the player. (*See Course Handicap*)

- **Hook:** A shot with an abrupt turn

- **Mulligan:** In casual play, a mulligan is a 'mistake' shot. Often, opponents will allow 1-2 mulligans every round.

- **Par:** *Professional Average Result*, the standard score for a hole or course

- **Rough:** Longest cut grass around the fairway

- **Spikes:** Shoes worn by golfers on the course, similar to cleats.

- **Sweet Spot:** The center of the golf club head which delivers the most power to the ball

- **Target Line:** The imaginary line from your ball to the target

- **Tee:** (1) area of the golf course from which the first shot per hole is made (also *teeing ground*); (2) the small spike on which a ball rests before the first shot

- **Trajectory:** The path of the ball once airborne

- **Yips:** A sudden run of bad luck or poor playing attributed to nervousness

Manufactured by Amazon.ca
Bolton, ON